South Middlesex

Edited by Heather Killingray

YoungWriters
First published in Great Britain in 2006 by:
Young Writers
Remus House
Coltsfoot Drive
Peterborough
PE2 9JX
Telephone: 01733 890066
Website: www.youngwriters.co.uk

SB ISBN 1 84602 469 2

Foreword

Young Writers was established in 1991 and has been passionately devoted to the promotion of reading and writing in children and young adults ever since. The quest continues today. Young Writers remains as committed to the nurturing of poetic and literary talent as ever.

This year's Young Writers competition has proven as vibrant and dynamic as ever and we are delighted to present a showcase of the best poetry from across the UK and in some cases overseas. Each poem has been selected from a wealth of *A Pocketful Of Rhyme* entries before ultimately being published in this, our fourteenth primary school poetry series.

Once again, we have been supremely impressed by the overall quality of the entries we have received. The imagination, energy and creativity which has gone into each young writer's entry made choosing the poems a challenging and often difficult but ultimately hugely rewarding task - the general high standard of the work submitted ensured this opportunity to bring their poetry to a larger appreciative audience.

We sincerely hope you are pleased with this final collection and that you will enjoy *A Pocketful Of Rhyme South Middlesex* for many years to come.

Contents

Isleworth Town Primary School

The Poems

Teddy Bear

Teddy bear lying on my comfy bed
In my pink bedroom where I comfortably sleep.

I was sleeping with my soft teddy
And left it on my comfy yellow bed.

I am going to my beautiful learning school
The next wonderful morning
And I can't take my teddy with me.

My teddy bear is very smooth
It's got a yellow ribbon
It's blue and it's like a bean bag
It's got a brown nose
An orange mouth and two purple ears.

Vrishni Badiali Silva (8)
Alexandra Junior School

The Python

A python I should not advise
It needs a doctor for its eyes
And has the measles every year.

However, if you feel inclined
To get one (to improve your mind)
And not merely for fashion.

Allow not music near its cage;
And when it flies into a rage,
Chastise it, most severely.

I had an aunt in Yucaton
Who brought a python from a man
And kept it for a pet.

She died because she never knew
These simple little rules of few.

The snake is still living yet!

Jaskiret Kaur Cheema (8)
Alexandra Junior School

The Magnificent Cat

The cat's fur is like a furry coat with black and white spots,
His eyes are like shimmering stars above the sky,
His tail is like a fluffy, sparkly pompom,
His paws a like a hard, rough stone in the sea,
He resembles a stormy night.

Kirhira Brown (8)
Edward Pauling Primary School

The Magnificent Dog

My dog is golden like the sun reflected in the river
Her fur is like a soft feather
Her eyes are like sparkling diamonds
Her paws are like smooth leather
I will miss her when she's gone, forever
And I'll always remember her.

Poppy Jones (8)
Edward Pauling Primary School

The Magnificent Dog

My dog is lovable and black and white like milk chocolate,
His nose is like a black, dark tunnel,
His eyes are like a thousand crystals glowing in the dark,
His teeth are enormous, like a rhino's horn,
His tail is like a wriggly worm,
He resembles a rhino.

Reece Roberts (9)
Edward Pauling Primary School

My Magnificent Fish

My fish is gold like the sun,
His tail is like the waves of the sea,
His scales shimmer like the sun shining on thousands of silver bars,
When I go to feed him, he always comes up to the top
And waits for the food.

Liam Williams (9)
Edward Pauling Primary School

The Magnificent Dog

My dog is as red as a rose,
Her nose is like a wet winter's day,
Her fur is like a soft pillow,
Her tail is like a wiggly worm,
She looks cute with a face so soft
And has eyes as brown as a tree.

Chloe Hamilton (8)
Edward Pauling Primary School

The Magnificent Dog!

My dog is black like melting dark chocolate,
His bark is like a broken record,
His tail is like a fan giving out a breeze to the flowers and grass,
His eyes are like shimmering pearls,
He resembles a guard dog,
I will take him for lovely long walks.

Brooke Cheeseman (9)
Edward Pauling Primary School

My Magnificent Puppy

My puppy is a little rascal, like a normal person,
His fur is like a soft, comfy cushion,
His eyes are like glamorous stars in the sky,
His tail is like a little curved seashell,
He resembles a little rascal and he is always very naughty,
He is very little and fluffy, like a fat bar of chocolate,
I will always look after him.

Charlotte Scotts (9)
Edward Pauling Primary School

The Magnificent Dog

My dog is as white as a piece of paper
His face is screwed up like a screwed up piece of paper
His eyes are like diamonds shining in the dark
In his heart he is a very good boy and one talented dog
I think he is the best! Ever!
He plays rough with the ball
His name is Harry
He guards my family
Most of all, he is a loving, caring dog and I love him!

Josh Sutch (9)
Edward Pauling Primary School

Anger Poem

I am angry,
But not guilty,
I'm hot-tempered
And everyone can see
When I'm angry, I get into a rage,
I shout at people,
Doesn't matter what's their age.

I get angry when someone annoys me,
I tell them to get lost and leave me be,
I am beyond annoyed and vexed,
I wonder what will happen next.

Kamilah Ramzan (11)
Hounslow Town Primary School

Anger Poem

When I feel angry,
I feel hot-tempered,
It's like the rage bursts like a volcano,
It makes you do so much.

I feel so furious,
I feel so frustrated,
I feel like I want to be all alone,
I have a fear that gets me angry.

When I see the colour red,
It feels like there's nothing but anger,
I get a red face
And that's when I get angry.

I feel so annoyed when I'm angry,
I feel so upset,
I feel like getting other's attention,
Anger makes you cry, it makes you do so much.

Simran Sagoo (10)
Hounslow Town Primary School

Anger Poem

I am vexed because of this
My best friend left and she I miss
I'm seeing red
I feel like I'm dead
I really miss her so
Why did her parents make her go?
I'm crying, I'm sad
I feel really bad,
Infuriated, infuriated
That's how I feel
That's how I feel, that's how I feel!

Nikita Goyale (11)
Hounslow Town Primary School

Anger Poem

Anger is a feeling that makes me upset,
For the things I've wanted, but cannot get,
Anger brings me hatred and rage,
You shouldn't feel it at any kind of age.

Domestic violence brings crime,
Luckily anger doesn't last for a long time,
Annoying, hot-tempered me,
Why just can't I be free?

Jasmine Kharod (11)
Hounslow Town Primary School

Anger Poem

I have so much anger in me
It's inside and hard to see
I feel frustrated, I don't know what to do
I run to my house, I never think things through
I am sweating, the anger controls my life
I am in a corner with a knife
Should I commit suicide or not?
Might as well
Because once I die, I will be in Hell and rot
I don't know what I did, I was out of control
God, please bless my soul.

Courtnie Greene (10)
Hounslow Town Primary School

Anger Poem

When I'm angry
I huff and puff
People tell me, 'Don't be rough'
I won't be rough, I'll be tough.

Anger isn't cool
So lose it or you'll look a fool
Anger is bad
Because people end up sad
And that is my poem for you!

Azfar Doshi (11)
Hounslow Town Primary School

The Anger Inside Me

Raging temper, seeing red,
Furious, resentful, killing my head.
Crying, frustrated, feeling vexed,
Outraged, splenetic exasperation
Flowing through my head.
Animosity, anguish, violence and death
Are four things to fear
Or you'll be next.

Ieuan Furborough (11)
Hounslow Town Primary School

Anger Poem

Everybody gets angry sometimes,
Everyone hitting and screaming.
When I'm angry sometimes I keep it inside,
Anger is not good, sometimes it's emotional,
The world gets angry at war.

Who wants to be angry?
But sometimes it's the only way
You can express yourself.
You can keep your anger inside
And be quiet and silent.
What's the point in being angry?
Only be angry for a good reason.

Chloe Kane (10)
Hounslow Town Primary School

Anger Poem

I am angry because I lose things
I'm so furious, I throw things around the room
When I feel angry, I really feel mad
When I'm in a rage, I feel that I'm in a grave
When I see red, I feel hot around my head.

Jai Pearce (11)
Hounslow Town Primary School

Violence

Violence rushes through streets and houses,
You can't stop violence.

Violence will wreck our happiness and kindness,
It spreads quickly like a fire in a house.

Violence is burning all your loved ones,
You need to talk to someone,
Fight back and you never know,
It may slowly drift away.

Sonika Pankhania (10)
Hounslow Town Primary School

Violence

Violence stomping through people
Breaking people's hearts like a tree branch snapping
Everything it touches turns to fear
When you feel it around
You try and move out of the way
But safety and security disappears
Like a tear dropping on the ground.

Tiffany Power (10)
Hounslow Town Primary School

Anger

Anger is a feeling that comes from within
It torments you and your kin
Avoid anger 'cause it's a sin

Anger comes from frustration
Anger's source is irritation
Anger can lead to devastation

Anger can make you sad
Anger can make you mad
Anger is very bad
But we all get angry, I don't know why, ask your dad

Anger isn't right
So don't get into a fight
Anger isn't cool
So avoid it and don't be a fool.

Vaibhav Agarwal (11)
Hounslow Town Primary School

Dealing With Anger

Anger reminds me of blood spitting in your face,
Anger is a clenched fist in your face,
My mind is blank, like the light switch turning off,
The world is against me,
I'm out of control
I want revenge!

Grown up, well, nearly grown up, out of childish behaviour,
It's like I'm calm and at peace with myself,
And I try to listen,
When I'm angry, I hold my breath
And grit my teeth!

Chuab Ahmed (10)
Hounslow Town Primary School

Respect Rules

R espect is good
E qual to great
S hare with others
P eople love it when you are kind
E very day be kind to people
C aring about other people
T each others to respect.

Hannah Rachel Lucy Jones (9)
Hounslow Town Primary School

Violence

Violence is spreading like spilt blood,
Roughly hurting kindness.
Violence is spreading,
Spreading slowly and darkly through other people.
Violence is brutality,
Ticking slowly,
In the wind.
Violence is lightning,
Breaking the darkness,
But violence doesn't get scared,
The people who spread it are cowards,
Will it stop as the darkness fades away?

Bilal Bhatti (10)
Hounslow Town Primary School

Learning To Respect Week

R is for respect
E is for everyone to show respect
S is for show respect
P is for people showing manners
E is for everybody showing kindness
C is for co-operating
T is for trying your best.

Kuldeep Daworaz (9)
Hounslow Town Primary School

Respect

R is for *r*espect that you show
E is for *e*veryone should be treated equally
S is for *s*howing manners and respect
P is for *p*eople should be kind
E is for *e*veryone should be treated fairly
C is for *c*aring for others
T is for *t*alking kindly to everyone.

Raashi Chavan (10)
Hounslow Town Primary School

Respect

R is for *r*espect
E is for *e*veryone to show respect
S is for *s*howing respect
P is for *p*eople that show manners
E is for *e*veryone sharing
C is for *c*o-operating
T is for *t*ry to respect.

Leah Wentzell (10)
Hounslow Town Primary School

Food, Glorious Food

Strawberry, chocolate, vanilla cake
All these cakes you just should bake.

Cold drinks, fizzy drinks, delicious drinks
Very, very tasty people think.

Tasty sugar, tea and coffee
With just a small hint of toffee.

Many, many desserts with cream on top
Just don't spill or you will mop.

Very, very good food, so tasty
I know I like it, especially pastry.

Nishali Karunatilleke (8)
Hounslow Town Primary School

Respect Poem

This week we are learning to respect
So put in some effort to do your best.

My grandad says respect to the elders
And love to the younger
In that way you can control your anger.

Respect to humans, respect to nature
And always respect another's culture.

Try to be happy, try to be kind
On success' ladder you'll never stay behind.

'Live and let live' is the motto we should have
In that way we will always be happy,
No one will be sad.

Parmvir Shallon (9)
Hounslow Town Primary School

Garden

My garden has beautiful flowers,
But my friend's garden has none!
My garden hasn't got a single weed,
But my friend's garden has loads!
My garden has lovely, fruitful trees,
But my friend's garden hasn't got any!
My garden has delicious strawberry bushes,
But my friend's garden has got brown!
My garden's got great things in it,
But my friend's garden hasn't got very many nice things in it.

Saima Haq
Hounslow Town Primary School

Poem Of Anger!

I did a crime, it was not my fault
I am annoyed because it's not my fault
You'd better back off because I am going to swear and not care
I'll huff and puff and keep myself tough
Wherever I go, I see red,
I do not know what to do.

Harshpal Singh (11)
Hounslow Town Primary School

Snow Storm

Grab your coat
Wear your scarf
Don't delay
The blizzard is coming!

Put on the heaters
Put on your hats
Don't delay
The blizzard is coming!

Wear your gloves
Put on your scarves
Don't delay
The blizzard is coming!

Vishnaka Muraleetharan (8)
Hounslow Town Primary School

Food, Glorious Food

Strawberry milkshake and crunchy pies
Veggie burgers and extra fries

Cheesy Doritos with salsa sauce
Rice and curry for main course

A lovely sundae with mint ice cream
Eating crunchy cake in my dream.

Kruti Vora (9)
Hounslow Town Primary School

All I Want To Do In Life

All I want to do in life is
Spread my wings and fly
I will never ever give up
Until I touch the sky

All I want to do in life is
Go to the moon and back
I will never ever give up
Until I'm right on track

All I want to do in life is
Swim in the deepest sea
I will never ever give up
Until I'm completely free

But now I'm getting older
And can't do many things
It might as well be better
As then I can grow wings.

Alice Dean (9)
Isleworth Town Primary School

Seasons

Autumn is the time
Trees shed their leaves
Animals sleep
Mist rises
Gardener sighs
Locks up his shed
Flower bed
Sleeps softly
It's quiet here
It's quiet.

Winter is the time
Everyone shivers
The rivers
Freeze
Snow rabbits
Snow foxes
They're all about
In feathered fur
It's cold here
It's cold.

Spring is the time
Chicks hatch
New life blossoms
The world is alive
Busy bustle
Pushing about
Egg hunt
Searching around
It's life again
It's life.

Summer is the time
Bright green leaves
Sweltering
No breeze
Anymore
Cold lemonade
School holiday
Swimming pool
It's hot again
It's hot.

Joey Yu (10)
Isleworth Town Primary School

Spring

As I run through the fields in the soft breeze of springtime,
Each blade of grass ripples like the sea's gentle wave.
Daisies and bluebells dance all around me,
To the soft, gentle wind they are simply just slaves.

As I gaze at the blue sky, so clear and so vivid,
The yellow sun glows like a lantern so warm.
Birds singing in trees up above me,
Winter's so far off - no sign of a storm.

As I touch the soft petals on each of the flowers,
The velvety feeling just warms me inside.
So that's why today, in the warm breeze of springtime,
It's such fun, it's such fun to be outside!

Ellen Plant (9)
Isleworth Town Primary School

My Pets

Once I got a tiger
But my mum said he was too vicious
So I gave him back to the zoo.

So I got some mice
But my dad said that they were too mischievous
So I put them back in the wall.

So I got a cat
But my uncle said that he kept on stealing his teeth
So I gave him back to the lady next door.

So I got a dog
But my gran said he kept stealing her wig
So I gave him back to the blind man across the road.

Saskia Loiola (10)
Isleworth Town Primary School

The Vampire Cat

The vampire cat has big red eyes,
Don't go near him or you're in for a surprise.
The vampire cat is simply unique,
His fur is so shiny and ever so sleek.
The vampire cat is scared of the sun,
As soon as it comes out, he always runs.
The vampire cat has big long claws
And also fangs that need applause.
The vampire cat disappears in the fog,
His owner's got rats and warts of a frog.
The vampire cat is a hunting professional,
His fuel is lightning, so his bite is electrical.
The vampire cat eats rats and birds,
The people who try to find him are real nerds.
The vampire cat listens to the wolves,
When the night comes he licks the skulls.
The vampire cat is better off alone,
Then the people who do not find him, will not moan.

Alice Williams (10)
Isleworth Town Primary School

Love

Love is a feeling in your heart
When two people can't be kept apart
You feel happy on a cloudy day
And nothing can take that feeling away
You hear birds chirping in the trees
And you smell blossom falling from the trees.

Sinead Tomlin (10)
Isleworth Town Primary School

Love

Love is like a touch of an angel
Love smells like perfume
Love looks like happiness
Love feels like a nice soft pillow.

Michael Yates (10)
Isleworth Town Primary School

Cyclones

Any type of cyclone puts you in danger
They are able to crush 100 mangers.
For lunch they devour houses
Leaving nothing but a mouse.
It moves like the wind
With absolutely no mind.

Daniel Mullin (9)
Isleworth Town Primary School

Books

Some books are soft,
Some books are hard,
Some books are made of fabric,
Some books are made of card.

Some books have pictures,
Some books have words,
Some books have animals,
Some books have birds.

Some books are fun,
Some books are scary,
Some books are good,
Some books are hairy.

Some books start,
Some books end,
Some books finish,
Some books you cannot mend.

Phoebe Maclean (9)
Isleworth Town Primary School

Seasons

Summer is a warm season,
The golden ball shining,
Ice creams melting quickly,
Beaches full up with people.

Footprints moulded in the sand,
Children playing in the sea,
Summer is a hot feeling,
Everyone enjoys it!

Summer is cool!

Nerissa Louise Panton (9)
Isleworth Town Primary School

Books

B ooks are enjoyable
O h they are fantastic
O h they really are interesting
K ids love them
S o you should read them all.

Sukhminder Randhowa (10)
Isleworth Town Primary School

Fear

F ear is the scariest thing
E verybody in the world hates fear
A t any time fear will strike at you
R ound, across and straight, fear is any shape.

Mohammed Harb (10)
Isleworth Town Primary School

Book Week!

B ooks are brilliant
O h my they're magical
O nly the people who read books have fun
K ids love to read them

W e love to read them and so should you
E xciting is what they are
E veryone would like them if they tried
K nowledge is what kids get from them and they are . . .

Books!

Harry Hall (10)
Isleworth Town Primary School

Winter

Winter is my season,
I have more than one reason,
It is frosty and beautiful
And the wind seizes to pull.

Whoever says I don't like spring,
Well then, they must not know a thing,
Autumn and summer, I like too,
But winter is sensational, what about you?

Ricky Dosanjh (10)
Isleworth Town Primary School

My Pet Jester

J umping
E nergetically
S tar of
T omorrow
E verything he does is . . .
R eally *cute!*

Louise Phillips (10)
Isleworth Town Primary School

Seasons!

Autumn
It's autumn already so I'd better wrap up warm,
Soon there may be a big storm!
The golden trees will sway
And the leaves will fly away, away, away!
I think I should stay inside
And wait till winter to go for a glide!

Winter
Winter is the time when Christmas is near,
Listen to the cards, can you hear?
The glisten of the floor when the snow sprinkles
The sound of the ice tinkles.
But, oh no, the snow seems to melt
As spring arrives!

Spring
Spring is the time when the flowers grow
And the sun shines brightly so . . .
Let's go outside and maybe hide
We could run around and around
Under the golden sun, but when spring is done
We don't have to wait till next time
Because there is a sign saying, *Summer Is On Its Way*!

Summer
Summer is the time when we all go off on a holiday,
The sun's hot but we still have fun!
We go on the sand and get in the sea,
When we're at the park, we can climb the tree!
It gets quite cold and it starts to rain
So go back home, onto the plane,
Now we're home, it's autumn again!

Sophie Jackson (10)
Isleworth Town Primary School

Happy

H appy is a feeling
A lways when you're having fun
P ersonality is what you show
P leased to see people
Y ou have fun.

Christopher Farnan (11)
Isleworth Town Primary School

Holidays

Holidays could be fun
There will be a hot beach
What you eat would be in a bun
You don't go to school and do a speech
The lovely sun will rise in your face
You can feel the air so warm
You stay for a week and at the end you pack your suitcase
So goodbye, you don't need to fill a form in.

Jordan Morris (9)
Isleworth Town Primary School

Riddle

I can rhyme but not rhyme if you don't want to,
I can be anything you want me to be about,
I am all around you if you think
What am I?

Rowland Charles Evans (10)
Isleworth Town Primary School

Love

Love feels like a soft cushion
Loves smells like roses
Love sounds like a harp
Love looks like the colour pink.

Bradley Bardowell (9)
Isleworth Town Primary School

Winter

W inter is when the leaves flow
I n winter the children play in the snow
N o more leaves in the trees
T ime to play now, just you and me
E veryone is now playing outside
R unning all about with no one inside.

Belma Jakupovic (9)
Isleworth Town Primary School

Care

People are dying in the world,
Could we help them?
Have you got a heart?
People are dying can't you see
You could be a hero
Just give something.

Charlie Moore (10)
Isleworth Town Primary School

Friends

Wherever you go,
If there is a helping hand,
Then I guess so,
If you believe in your heart,
Then follow the way,
You may see or know anyone
Let's just say,
Like Sinead she's number one
And if you need someone to talk to
Go to her, Zoe
She's number two
And if you need someone to play with
Go to her, Sinead
Let's not forget Phoebe, Alice D and W Belma too
I'll be back soon.

Vikki Tilby (9)
Isleworth Town Primary School

The Best Nan Ever!

The greatest nan ever,
Isn't a feather.
Not a rock,
Or a flock.
She lives around the corner,
Her name isn't Lorna.

Her name isn't Danni,
Or Annie.
Debbie's the name
And winning isn't her fame.

Her husband isn't Harry,
Or Barry.
It's Leon the most fantastic grandad ever.

Debbie has two sons and two daughters,
Steven, Scott, Leona and Tanya.

I love my nan and I know you do too,
She has had the flu.

She's the best nan anyone could have
But better!

Charlotte Louise Crome (10)
Isleworth Town Primary School

Scared

S cared is a feeling
C aused by being frightened
A horrible feeling
R eally frightened
E verybody's hiding
D etermined to ruin your life.

Amy Smith (10)
Isleworth Town Primary School

My Poem

My hair's beautiful
And my eyes are colourful,
My friends are friendly
And my family are cheerful,
Now I'm just going to say this once
So listen up,
I don't want to be bullied
And I want some friends to play with me tomorrow.

Suman Kumar (10)
Isleworth Town Primary School

School Is Great

School is great,
So don't be late,
You can meet a very good mate,
Her name is Kate,
She walks nicely through the gate,
You can take her out for a date.

Oliver Bowles (7)
Isleworth Town Primary School

Squeeze

We love to squeeze bananas
We love to squeeze ripe plums
But when we are feeling sad
We love to squeeze our mums.

Nakul Plaha (7)
Isleworth Town Primary School

If I Wasn't Me

If I wasn't me
I would be
A ninja turtle
I would come to school
Jumping from building to building
With my friends on my back
The teacher would say my name
And I would say, 'Here Miss!'

Taylor Thorne (8)
Isleworth Town Primary School

If I Wasn't Me

If I wasn't me
I'd rather be
King Kong
I'd come to school
Jumping onto the building
And the teacher would say,
'King Kong, come in now.'
And I'd say, 'Coming!'

Jordan Dale (7)
Isleworth Town Primary School

If I Wasn't Me

If I wasn't me
I'd rather be Spider-Man
I'd come to school
With my friends on my shoulders
The teacher would say, 'Spider-Man?'
And I'd say, 'Here Miss.'

If I wasn't me
I'd rather be a crazy chimpanzee
I'd come to school from tree to tree
The teacher would say, 'Crazy chimpanzee?'
And I'd say, 'Here Miss.'

Ciara Coen-D'Arcy (8)
Isleworth Town Primary School

If I Wasn't Me

If I wasn't me
I would rather be
The bindi babe Geena
I would travel in a limousine
I would be at the wheel
With my friends drinking pop at the back
At school Miss would say, 'Bindi babe Geena?'
And I would say, 'Yes Miss.'

Geena Ludhra (8)
Isleworth Town Primary School

Books

Books, books, books
I love books
So many books to choose from
In books you hear stories about hooks and keys
And maybe about big bumblebees
Girls who are very clever
And mad machines going *hoop, hoop, hever!*
Oh, how I love books
In a book you hear stories about horrid ladies,
Who only care about their looks,
Oh how I love books!

Molly Mills (7)
Isleworth Town Primary School

Countryside

Countryside so green
Countryside so quiet
Countryside so packed with animals
Countryside smells like nature all around you
In the countryside
People come to see the lovely nature.

Morgan Yates (9)
Isleworth Town Primary School

If I Wasn't Me

If I wasn't me
I'd rather be
Bart Simpson.

I'd come to school
By skateboard
The teacher would say, 'Bart Simpson?'
I'd say, 'Here Miss.'

James Hall (8)
Isleworth Town Primary School

I Wish!

I wish I had a dog,
I wish I had one *soooo* much,
I wish I had one that would play ball
And come when I called.

I wish I had a rabbit,
I wish I had one *soooo* much,
I wish I had one that would cuddle me when I wished
And ate off a dish.

I wish I had a doll,
I wish I had one *soooo* much,
I wish I had one that would
Play with me when I wanted
Or let me dress her.

I wish I had a cat,
I wish I had one *soooo* much,
I wish I had one that would purr
When I stroked it
And would sit when I wanted it to sit.

Now I have all those things,
But my dog keeps chewing the curtains,
Or chasing the cat
And my rabbit won't eat off a dish
Or cuddle me when I wish
And my doll doesn't fit any of my clothes,
Also my cat doesn't purr when I stroke it.

I don't want any of these . . .
I want a snake!

Hannah Blayden (10)
Isleworth Town Primary School

Books

Some books have been awaken
And some books have been taken.

Some books are flappy
And some books are happy.

Some books are hard
And some books have card.

Books are for reading
And don't need feeding.

Some books are scary
And some books are hairy.

I hope you can mend
The books that aren't meant to bend.

I know you swear
But please care.

Lincoln Williamson (10)
Isleworth Town Primary School

Fashion

F ashion is something you should have
A t parties you'll look so glam
S eeing people that are dull and bad
H ow can they take it being so sad
I love fashion, so should you
O n school days too
N ever let people bring you down, if they do just call them a clown!

Movarid Ahmadi (10)
Isleworth Town Primary School

Moon Dance

If I sleep by day
And dance by night.
If the stars are my friends,
They are dim by my light.
If the clouds are my bed
And the sky's my home.
If I rise in the west
And to the east I roam.
If the world goes quiet
When I'm at my greatest height.
If the owl only flies
Like a grey forgotten kite.
If my light is pale
And my friend's is yellow, bright.
If her world is golden
And mine is silvery white.
Can you tell me which of us is right?
For if my light is silvery white,
I am the moon, is that not right?

Desanka Markovic (10)
Isleworth Town Primary School

Seasons!

Autumn is the time,
When the leaves turn brown
And fall to their new home.
It is the time,
When the animals sleep,
The flowers in their bed,
The sky turns grey.
The grass glitters and gleams
With a shimmering sheen.
More lights appear,
More lights appear.

Spring is the time
When the flowers open
Their beautiful colours
Start to appear.
The animals start to wake up,
Prancing and dancing.
It is the time
Where the birds
Start to chirp,
Birds start to chirp.

Winter is the time,
When the gleaming snow falls,
The moon is like a bright ball.
It is the time
To put up the Christmas tree
And watch the beautiful lights
It is very cold,
Very cold.

Summer is the time,
Where the dresses and shorts appear,
It is the time
When the beaches are full,
Ice creams are sold out
It is very hot,
Very hot.

Layla Ziadi
Isleworth Town Primary School

The Worries

The worries in my head
They give me a fright
The worries in my head
They don't do what's right
The worries in my head
They are scary
The worries in my head
They make me hairy.

Simmy Greaves (8)
Isleworth Town Primary School

Pie

Pie is a lovely treat
That we eat after a meal
Pie is a lovely treat
That we eat when we feel.
We can eat it with ice cream
We can eat it with custard
You can eat it with a spoon
But still it is supreme.
You can eat it when you're sad
You can eat it when you're mad
You can eat it with your dad.
You can eat it while on the move
You can eat it when you're groovy
But the whole point is
You can eat it with a smoothie.

DeDe Olatunji (10)
Isleworth Town Primary School

If I Wasn't Me

If I wasn't me
I'd rather be
A whale
Or a crazy monkey.

I'd come to school
And I would swim
The teacher would say, 'Whale?'
And I would say, 'Here Miss.'

Lucy Bennett (7)
Isleworth Town Primary School

If I Wasn't Me

If I wasn't me, I'd rather be a cat in a hat,
If I wasn't me, I'd rather be a Bratz,
If I wasn't me, I'd rather be a pop star,
If I wasn't me, I'd rather be an art girl,
If I wasn't me, I'd rather be a pearl.

Meshabel Nakayiwa (7)
Isleworth Town Primary School

If I Wasn't Me

If I wasn't me
I'd rather be
A shark
I'd come to school
By jumping from each puddle
With my friends on my dorsal fin!

If I wasn't me
I'd rather be
Chief Brody
From the movie, 'Jaws'.

If I wasn't me
I'd rather be
A frog
I'd get to school
By hop, hop, hopping.

If I wasn't me
I'd rather be
ET the extraterrestrial
I'd come to school by spaceship
With friends in the passenger seats!

Louis Kelly (8)
Isleworth Town Primary School

If I Wasn't Me

If I wasn't me
I'd rather be
'Cat In The Hat
I'd come to school
In a red and white hat
With my friends on my back
The teacher would say, 'Cat In The Hat?'
And I'd say, 'Here Miss.'

Georgia Brewster (8)
Isleworth Town Primary School

Lunchtime

At lunch the bell goes ding
All the boys and girls sing
As we go in and wash our hands
The dinner ladies cook with pans
We line up for our dinner, ready to eat
And then we go to our seats.

Jessica McLaughlin (7)
Our Lady of the Rosary RC Primary School

Lunchtime

At lunchtime we line up fast
And go in with a blast
To wash our hands
As the dinner ladies check the pans
We eat our lunch
In a bunch.

Emanuel Andrade
Our Lady of the Rosary RC Primary School

Lunchtime

At lunchtime we go in with a blast
We eat our lunch so fast
So we don't be late
We go outside for some fun
And hope there is sun.

Barnaby Baines (8)
Our Lady of the Rosary RC Primary School

The Wobbling Race

Two jellies had a wobbling race
To see who was the wobbliest
Then the sun came out and melted them
And made them both the dribbliest!

Jordan Mancienne-Ponwaye
St Lawrence's RC Primary School, Feltham

The Castle Cat Attack!

The castle cats attack the rats,
To keep the corridors clear,
To stop the mess the rascals make,
When they run with fear!
They nibble and scratch and chew at the latch
Of all the castle doors,
They slide on floors to escape the claws,
That's attached to the furry paws,
The cats keep the rats at bay,
By order of the king
And when they have a good day's work
It's supper with a grin!

Bradley Fox (9)
St Lawrence's RC Primary School, Feltham

Laughter

Laughter is yellow like the sun
Laughter feels giggly
Laughter reminds you of funny
Laughter smells like perfume on a flower
Laughter sounds like snakes
It tastes like laughs.

Bryony Thomas (8)
St Lawrence's RC Primary School, Feltham

Love

Love is red like your heart
It's full of love and kindness
It feels hot
It reminds you that someone loves you and hugs you
It smells like perfume
It looks like flowers
It sounds like the sea
It tastes like sweets.

Carole El Baba (8)
St Lawrence's RC Primary School, Feltham

Fun

Fun is yellow like the sunlight
It feels like a bright light
It reminds me of a good day
It smells like popcorn
It looks like a light
It sounds like laughter
It tastes like sweets.

Leon Amoah (8)
St Lawrence's RC Primary School, Feltham

Laughter

Laughter is sky-blue like the sky
It feels like someone's tickling you
It reminds you of a hot summer's day
It smells like the perfume of flowers
It looks like joy
It sounds like the birds singing
It tastes like nice, juicy sweets.

Toni-Louise Hopkins (8)
St Lawrence's RC Primary School, Feltham

Happiness

Happiness is green like grass
Happiness feels amazing
Happiness reminds you of fun
Happiness smells nice
Happiness looks like magic
Happiness sounds like fun
Happiness tastes like sweets.

Abel Testagasbar (8)
St Lawrence's RC Primary School, Feltham

Happiness

Happiness is yellow like the sun
It feels as soft as a moon
It reminds me of a soft bear
It smells like a beautiful rose
It looks like a calm voice
It sounds like the grass moving
It tastes joyful.

Jessica Boylett (8)
St Lawrence's RC Primary School, Feltham

Laughter

Laughter is blue like the sea
It feels like joy and fun
It reminds me of great times
It smells like the perfume of flowers
It sounds like birds singing
It tastes like lovely chocolates.

Laughter is good!

Jade Cook (8)
St Lawrence's RC Primary School, Feltham

Sadness

Sadness is grey like a black day
It feels like I don't exist
It reminds me of me passing away
It smells like a gone-off lemon
It looks like a puddle of water
It sounds like a tap running out
It tastes like burning in your mouth.

Christopher Alexandre (8)
St Lawrence's RC Primary School, Feltham

Friendship

Friendship is purple like lavender
It feels like a lovely day pouring on you
It reminds you of your very first teddy bear
It smells like a bunch of flowers
It looks like everyone cares
It sounds like everyone laughing
It tastes like a craft of lemons.

Shauna Long (8)
St Lawrence's RC Primary School, Feltham

Roses

Roses are red like the first colour of the rainbow
It feels like soft fresh air
It reminds me of violets
It smells like strawberries
It looks like a rainbow
It sounds like the waves from far, far away
It tastes like strawberry trifle.

Chloe Sewell (8)
St Lawrence's RC Primary School, Feltham

Happiness

Happiness is orange like the sun
It feels smooth and soft
It reminds me of blue sky and green grass
It smells joyful
It looks like the sunrise
It sounds peaceful
It tastes like joy.

Teri Pereira (8)
St Lawrence's RC Primary School, Feltham

Happiness

Happiness is green like the green grass in the park
It tastes like seaweed in the sea
It sounds like a blast of wind in the sky
It feels like fun at the park
It smells like perfume
It looks like people laughing in the playground.

Gabrielle Macedo (8)
St Lawrence's RC Primary School, Feltham

Love

Love is red like a red, beautiful rose shining in the leaves
Love sounds like a dove singing
Love tastes like fruit, juicy and sweet
Love looks like doves together, singing
Love smells like roses gleaming
Love feels like smooth cushions
Love reminds me of helping people and sharing things.

Francesca Tarrant (8)
St Lawrence's RC Primary School, Feltham

Love

Love is pink like roses blowing in the sun
It looks like a heart gleaming in the sun
It sounds like a bird flying in the air
It tastes like sausages sizzling in a pan
It feels like a romantic day out
It reminds me of a romantic day at the beach.

Emma Davie (8)
St Lawrence's RC Primary School, Feltham

Anger

Anger is red like a devil
It sounds like a terrible dragon
It tastes like fresh meat from a shark
It smells like a red ball
It looks like a black body with big horns
It feels like a soft teddy in my mum's room
It reminds me of when my soft teddy went in the wash.

Stefan Krieger (8)
St Lawrence's RC Primary School, Feltham

Love

Love is like a pink, gleaming heart
It feels like happiness in our heart
It reminds me of romantic things
It sounds like a pumping heart
It tastes like a night on the sea
It smells like laughter in the air
It looks like two people running in the park.

Reagan Thomas (8)
St Lawrence's RC Primary School, Feltham

Sadness

Sadness is blue like rain from a cloud
It sounds sad but it's sometimes loud
It tastes like salty water
It feels like you're lonely and not near anybody
It reminds me of tears dropping in my tea
It smells like nothing but tears
It looks like tiny water dripping near.

Celina Basa (8)
St Lawrence's RC Primary School, Feltham

Fun

Fun is yellow like the sun burning in the sky
It feels like the burning sun
It tastes like a yellow banana
It reminds me of someone cooking
It smells like brown mushrooms
It looks like a yellow machine
It sounds like crashing cars in the street.

Harrold Galapate (8)
St Lawrence's RC Primary School, Feltham

My Motherland

Even when I was little
To my mind, I have always wondered
Living in another far country
But of course with my own family.

Now I've had the chance
In this big country of Great Britain
With a different way of living
Far from what I used to be doing.

Throughout our stay here, it's stable
I would still want to go back home
Because there is no comparison
To be in my only home, my motherland.

Ivan Renz Villanueva (10)
St Lawrence's RC Primary School, Feltham

Happiness

Happiness is orange like a day at the beach
Happiness smells like a cold, snowy storm that never stops
It looks like shadows of children playing with their families
It sounds like a bundle of elephants that are banging together
It tastes like a variety of my favourite foods
It feels like some friendly ghosts that are dancing
It reminds me of a day at the beach with my family and friends.

Bethany Wigmore (8)
St Lawrence's RC Primary School, Feltham

Sport

Football is fun,
Football is great,
I love football,
I play it with my mates.

Rugby is hard,
Rugby is tough,
To play rugby,
You've got to be rough.

Golf is calm,
Golf is cool,
All you have to do,
Is hit the little white ball.

Tennis is fast,
Tennis is fun,
Roger Federer
Is the world's number one.

Jake Wigmore (11)
St Lawrence's RC Primary School, Feltham

Break time = Football

Girls and boys
It's break time
Football here we go
It doesn't matter
If you win or lose
But if you score a goal
Everyone screams and shouts
We're winning, yes we are
Try and score another one
Then we'll win for sure!

Laura Walmsley (10)
St Lawrence's RC Primary School, Feltham

Ice Cream

I like ice cream a whole lot
It tastes good when days are hot
In a cone or on a dish
It would be my only wish.

Nicest on a sunny day
I like ice cream in every way
All the flavours, vanilla and choc
I just want to scoff the lot!

I love ice cream, yes I do
I don't want one scoop, I want two!
I love ice cream, yes I do
I love ice cream and so should you!

Leah Walsh (11)
St Lawrence's RC Primary School, Feltham

Why And What

Have you ever wondered
Why you're alive
Or if the universe rumbled
Would you still be alive?
Do you take your life for granted
Or do you love your life?
Because life is actually hard
Like trying to balance a knife.
Life is a pinch
Life is a punch
Life is everywhere.
Just like a plant seed
That grows here and there.
Just like a child
Aged five, four, three or two
That ends up as brave as a forty-year-old
And does not cry to go to the loo.
Life is you
Life is me
Life is everything
Don't you see?
Now you will figure out
That life is for living
And not for having doubts.
So I hope you like this poem
And think it's really kind
And maybe this little poem
Can help you change your mind.

Sophonias Getachew (11)
St Lawrence's RC Primary School, Feltham

I Love Football

On a Saturday morning,
I get up for football training,
Even when it's raining.

I run around the pitch,
Until I get a stitch,
When me and my mates start to ache
We take a little break
Back to the game
Where we all seek fame.

We are wet and tired
And our game is lame,
But we pull ourselves together
To play the Sunday game.

The whistle is blown
The game is over,
Now we can all go home.

Lee Curley (10)
St Lawrence's RC Primary School, Feltham

Time Goes Quick

When playing in the park
With all of my friends
We did not know the time
Until it was the end
The sun had gone down
The park was all dark
I was frightened and scared
I could not see any light.

Christopher Light (10)
St Lawrence's RC Primary School, Feltham

I Don't Like Writing Poems

I don't like writing poems
I think it's rather daft
They're really hard to think of
And try to make you laugh
Poems can be boring
Poems can be dull
I like the funny poems
The silly ones from the past.

Lorenzo Rossetti (10)
St Lawrence's RC Primary School, Feltham

In The Forest

In the forest there is a hunter as fearless as can be
In the forest there is a wolf as scary as can be
In the forest there is a bear as frightening as can be
In the forest there is a snake as poisonous as can be
Oh I hope, I really hope, that the snake, the hunter, the bear
and the wolf
Never fight or the forest will not be a forest anymore.

Ben Jowers (10)
St Lawrence's RC Primary School, Feltham

Imagine

The violet crystals float gently in a sea of tears,
Swaying one way and the other, smoothly in the cool air,
It calms me, this place, in times of loneliness and worry,
The calm breeze shoots through the white-topped,
glistening mountains.

Imagine

Emotions sink into the depth of the cold, clear sea,
The young, innocent children dance merrily,
Trampling across the emerald-green grass.

Imagine

But this dream fades away
And back to reality I go
Hey, it's not so bad!
Until . . .

Just imagine . . .

Siobhan Cadden (10)
St Lawrence's RC Primary School, Feltham

Sadness

Sadness is blue like a girl that is sad
And tears coming from her glowing eyes
It smells like the ocean waves going into the sand
It looks like the tropical palm trees blowing around
It tastes like sour chicken
It feels like the breeze blowing on my face
It reminds me of the happiness and joy that we have
In America, Switzerland, France and the Isle of Wight
It sounds like people crying.

Jessica Uwen (8)
St Lawrence's RC Primary School, Feltham

Anger

What colour is it?
Red is anger
It is dangerous
Like anger
It is red like a crocodile snapping
It sounds like a drum
What does it taste like?
Fresh shark meat
It smells like a red ball
Anger is red like a crocodile snapping
It sounds like a drum
It tastes like fresh meat from a shark
It sounds like a drum
It smells like bananas
It looks like a mean dog
It feels like you are sad
It reminds me of people who say sorry.

Jessica Heer (8)
St Lawrence's RC Primary School, Feltham

Little Red Riding Hood Vs The Bad Wolf

Well, you've heard the story of Little Red Riding Hood
Who lived in the neighbourhood
She said that she could
And wasn't sure if she should
Take the risk of walking through the wood.

In the wood it was very dark
Then Red Riding Hood heard a bark
'Listen,' the creature remarked
'My bite is worse than my bark
My teeth leave a mark.'

Little Red Riding Hood ran ahead
Wishing that she was in bed
Only to find when she got there
Her granny was there instead.

Suddenly Red Riding Hood could see
That something wasn't the way it should be
When she looked from the side of her eye
She let out an almighty cry.

For there in front of her eyes
Was a big surprise
It was the wolf in disguise
'Do you like pies?'
'No, I like children,' the wolf replied
'Argh!' Little Red Riding Hood cried.

In comes the woodcutter with his awful twin
Both bearing an enormous grin
The wolf was rubbing his chin
Thinking of sin
With a spin
He kicks the woodcutter's shin
But the awful twin
Pierces the wolf's skin.

When they opened his tummy
It was hilariously funny
To see Granny jump out with a bunny
In that fit of laughter
I suppose they lived happily ever after.

Eileen Igboanugo (9)
St Lawrence's RC Primary School, Feltham

Snail, Snail

Oh snail, snail,
Look at your beautiful, silver trail
You travel in the morning
And sleep at night
Oh snail, snail,
You're such a delight.

Lee Lauder (8)
St Lawrence's RC Primary School, Feltham

My Connor, The Gonna

There once was a boy called Connor
Who kissed the singer Madonna
She slapped him on the cheek
And called him a freak
And said, 'Goodbye, you're a gonna!'

Chris Nisbet (10)
St Lawrence's RC Primary School, Feltham

Fun

Fun is green like grass
It looks like angels playing football with you
It reminds you of all the parties you've had
It smells like marshmallows
It sounds like children playing in the park
It tastes like snowflakes on your tongue.

Jacob Bennett (8)
St Lawrence's RC Primary School, Feltham

Love

Love is red like someone is loving your heart
If feels hot around you
It reminds you of having been good
It smells like perfume
It looks like flowers
It sounds like the sea
It tastes like sweets.

Nikita Da Silva (8)
St Lawrence's RC Primary School, Feltham

Fun

Fun is yellow like the shining sun brightening the world
It feels like happiness in the sky
It reminds me of a sunny, shiny, fun day
It sounds like children playing and laughing
It tastes like chips
It smells like a smelly flower
It looks like children playing.

Christie McVay (8)
St Lawrence's RC Primary School, Feltham

Happiness

Happiness is sky-blue like a gleaming heart
It sounds like a crowd of happy people cheering with laughter
It tastes like a wobbly jelly of joy
It smells like the perfume of a rose
It looks like a rainbow of colours
It feels like the hot sun of fire with laughter
It reminds me of playing with my friends.

Caitlin Jordan (8)
St Lawrence's RC Primary School, Feltham

Santa, Santa, You Need To Go Shopping

Santa, Santa, you need to go shopping
Get something for the reindeer
Maybe this or that
Going down the aisles
Knocking down the tiles
Round the bend
Nearly at the end
To the till
Pay the bill
And that's the end of that!

Christopher Perryment (9)
St Lawrence's RC Primary School, Feltham

The Witch, Beast, Wizard And Hag

There was a little witch,
Who had a little itch,
Upon her hairy little back.

There was a stinking beast,
Who had a stinking feast,
In his stinking swamp.

There was a clever wizard,
Who had a clever lizard,
In his rusty, clever castle.

There was an old hag,
Who had an old bag,
Upon her wrinkly old shoulder.

Lydia Elliott (9)
St Lawrence's RC Primary School, Feltham

The Dragon's Lunch

Once upon a time on a sunny day
The dragon left the den to go and play
On his way he saw a girl and boy
And both of them were full of joy
When they saw the dragon
They jumped into a wagon
Then the wagon rolled down the hill
For one minute the dragon stood still
Then it flew down the hill breathing fire
Until he got caught in a telephone wire
Then he bit the wire and was free to fly
So he flapped his wings and flew into the sky
This time they had no chance to get away
The dragon picked them up and took them away
When he got them back to his den
He ate them up and that was the end of them.

Emma Beharie (9)
St Lawrence's RC Primary School, Feltham

Spring

When I hear the robins sing
I feel happy it is spring

Flowers blowing in the breeze
Rustling leaves in the trees

Squirrels scurrying across the lawn
A lazy cat lets out a yawn

Bumblebees buzz away
Collecting pollen for the day

Butterflies flap their colourful wings
With all the joy that spring brings

Spring is a time where we all feel free
Everyone loves spring, especially me!

Lauraine Etienne (10)
St Lawrence's RC Primary School, Feltham

Lost At Secondary School

School, OK, I'm up and in my uniform,
Time for the bus,
I can't miss it,
Right, now I'm here,
English first, let's hear a cheer,
But oh no, where are the English rooms?
Too late, hall patroller's taken me in,
'No wait, head teacher, I can explain,
It's, well, my first day
And I'm not used to the school.'
'Not used to the school,
It's not that hard,
Suppose a warning should do for now,
Once more, then *expelled* is the word for you,
For now an hour's detention should do.'
'Oh, thank you, Sir, I'm really grateful.'
'Goodbye now, hurry to class,
Quickly before I say
Go home
For now you are *expelled!'*

Abbey Tweedle (11)
St Lawrence's RC Primary School, Feltham

Sadness

Sadness is black like a dark shadow
It feels like a dark, dull, lonely day
It reminds me of the wind blowing me away
It sounds like lightning striking the ground
It tastes like sadness melting in your mouth
It smells like an odour invading your nose
It looks like a mountain going to explode.

John Francis Igboanugo (8)
St Lawrence's RC Primary School, Feltham

All Friends Are Different

My friends come in all shapes and sizes,
Some are sporty, some are wise,
Some have blonde hair, some have brown,
Some jump up and some sit down.
Boys and girls,
Big and small,
Some are short and some are tall.
Girls play on the climbing frames,
The boys like playing football games.
When I'm sad and feeling lonely,
I can call a special friend to be with me only.

Daniel Polley (10)
St Lawrence's RC Primary School, Feltham

Ghosts

Lots of people are scared of ghosts
They say, 'Ghosts are the things I fear most.'
How can they think ghosts are scary?
They're as kind and gentle as a magical fairy.

I'm talking about a ghost,
That comes in the night,
While everyone's in bed,
Tucked in tight.

He visits each house, one by one,
Every single night,
He gives the people of the house,
A ride in the moonlight.

He rides up high,
Right into the sky,
All the way to the moon,
Every night,
When he rides in the sky,
He uses a magical spoon!

So why be afraid of ghosts,
When they can be so kind?
I hope this poem about ghosts,
Made you change your mind.

Conor Bacon (10)
St Lawrence's RC Primary School, Feltham

The Fairy Surprise

Little do you know and little do you see
I have a poem written by thee
It's written with a pen
Made by hand
Nothing can stop this fairy and
What is this about you say?
It's fairies who float and dance by the bay.
They dance and sing and twirl and spin
They hide a surprise, waiting to be found
And hopefully crowned.
It's sweet with a hint of love
And once you've eaten you'll see a dove
It will sing to you and wait as they do
To be thanked and praised from all.

Rebecca O'Sullivan (10)
St Lawrence's RC Primary School, Feltham

Fun

Fun is yellow like the hot sun in the sky
It feels like a hot fun day at the park
It reminds me of happiness
It tastes like a sweet
It smells like the beach
It looks like the sun
It sounds like children giggling.

Jack Everett (8)
St Lawrence's RC Primary School, Feltham

My Extraordinary Friends

Cinder is as black as coal,
Sleek and shiny.
Patch is as white as snow,
All furry with blotches of grey.
Now let me tell you some more.

Cinder is petite and bright,
With short, black ears,
That stand up tall.
She has a minute nose,
That loves to be stroked and tickled.

Patch is a giant, but as timid as can be,
With long, white ears,
That droop down low.
She has a curious face,
With a nose that twitches.

These are my rabbits,
My two extraordinary friends.
Lovable, cuddly, amusing and fun,
Only small but with so much love.
How lucky I am,
To be blessed with these two.

Emily Ballantyne (11)
St Lawrence's RC Primary School, Feltham

Once I Brought My Pet Dinosaur To School!

Once I brought my pet dinosaur to school,
It was a really scary sight,
He picked up all the minibuses,
With all his strong might.
He ate them with a gollop,
Swallowing them down quickly,
Everyone ran away,
In his throat it was tickly.
He even ate the teachers,
He ate them all up!
He even drank their tea,
In a very big cup!
He stormed away,
Thinking he was cool,
Everyone except me,
Thought that he was a fool!

Lucy Joely Boylett (11)
St Lawrence's RC Primary School, Feltham

Laughter

Laughter is pink like rosy-pink cheeks
It feels like making myself play hide-and-seek
It reminds me of my happy times
It sounds like a comforting noise - mine
It tastes like a night on the sea
It looks like me
And it smells like everyone I see.

Charlotte Hatherley (8)
St Lawrence's RC Primary School, Feltham

Love

Love is pink like dust floating in the air
It feels like happiness in our hearts
It reminds me of romantic things
It sounds like your heart beating
It tastes like a first kiss
It looks like people laughing
It smells like shiny metal armour.

Daniel Perkis (8)
St Lawrence's RC Primary School, Feltham

Poems Made Easy

I've been asked to write a poem,
That could be published in a book,
But I'm finding it quite difficult,
For ideas and where to look.

I've asked my mum and dad for clues,
My brother makes it hard to choose,
They're no help at all to me,
So here I go, let's wait and see!

Each line is taking energy and time
And it's really hard to make things rhyme,
Poems are not easy, though people may think so,
Well, what I have to say to them is, 'Try and give it a go.'

People have their doubts that I can pull this off,
But their words I'll make them eat, with relish, what a scoff,
This poem is nearly over and I've enjoyed every bit,
I hope you all appreciate the effort that has gone into it.

Maria-Theresa Vidal (10)
St Lawrence's RC Primary School, Feltham

Laughter

Laughter is orange like a shiny orange
It sounds like Heaven having a playground
It tastes like ripe strawberries
It smells like free air
It looks like people being miserable and are free again
It feels like you can make a joke with everyone
It reminds me of the time I was born.

Kiana Doshoki (8)
St Lawrence's RC Primary School, Feltham

A Dog's Adventure

A dog was crossing the road,
Stopped there, he stood,
Looking left and right,
Waiting for a chance to cross to the other side.

Walking home he was, all alone,
Scared and hungry, he carried on,
Thinking of arriving soon,
To his owner's beloved home.

He was happy to be back,
To his family home, especially as he'd
Felt so loved and was lucky
And was proud of his life again.

Louis Dinis (11)
St Lawrence's RC Primary School, Feltham

Pink Carnation

She's cloaked in a svelte emerald gown,
Her delicate head surveys the candyfloss clouds in the azure sky,
Then gently tilts back down,
The zephyr nudges her softly, she tosses her dayglo head and sighs,
As the crisp, cool day draws on, an amber bee flits near,
She studies it intently and flashes a glimmer of a smile
And the caramel bee flutters closer and hums in her ear,
She sighs again deeply and glances wearily at the sundial,
Later on that day, a red admiral glides past,
She listens reluctantly to his words,
Carnation nods regretfully and looks downcast,
She allows her eyes to pass to the birds,
One falls dead with cold and she knows it's true, she starts to
droop and weep,
What her friends had warned her of was a fact;
It was now indeed time for the 'big sleep'.

Katie Hatherley (10)
St Lawrence's RC Primary School, Feltham

Talents

I have talents
You have talents
We all have talents, we do.
He has talents
She has talents
Babies have talents too.

Think and use your talents
As talents should be used
Because talents are not toys
And should not be abused.

I love my talent
You love your talent
We all love our talents, yes we do.
So make sure that ever in your life, no one gives you a boo
So enjoy your talent, even if it's in a pool,
Then sooner or later everyone will know you rule.

Abigail Getachew (9)
St Lawrence's RC Primary School, Feltham

Writing A Poem

What a big deal
You have to make it rhyme
Well, only sometimes
Although you can use any subject

Writing a poem
It's so hard
Make it interesting or funny
Whatever suits you
Writing a poem
I just wrote one!

Daniel Muranda (10)
St Lawrence's RC Primary School, Feltham

Football

Football on Sunday morning
My brother thinks it's very boring
He stays in bed
Dreaming instead
As we get to the match
The ref blows the whistle
And the rain starts to drizzle
We run for the ball
They don't get it at all
By the end it's 7-0
The game we have won
Oh, that was such a great thrill!

Andrew Billing (10)
St Lawrence's RC Primary School, Feltham

Hide-And-Seek

Hey, come and play with us, we're playing hide-and-seek
But remember, if you're counting, you must not peek.
'Who's playing?' did you ask? Shall I tell you who's here?
There are people from fairy tales that will come from far and near.
We've got Goldilocks, Cinderella, Tinkerbell too
And Ariel, the big bad wolf, I hope he doesn't scare you.
I will count and you will hide
There's three blind mice you have to guide.
If I find you, you are out
It doesn't matter, so please don't pout.
And when the game is finished, we'll all go home for tea
We'll play again tomorrow sometime, just you wait and see.

Deanna Lashbrook (10)
St Lawrence's RC Primary School, Feltham

My Dad

This is a poem about my dad
He is almost never sad

To me, he is a king
But he can't sing!

It doesn't matter, so be it
Because he is the opposite of a twit

He likes beer
You should hear his cheer!

He likes to bounce
But he's my dad, that's what counts!

James Durrans (9)
St Lawrence's RC Primary School, Feltham

Goldilocks

Hey there Goldilocks,
Are you wearing any frocks?

Yes, I have frocks,
Frocks in a great big box!

Hey there Goldilocks,
Where did you get your box?

I got my box from a store,
On the top floor.

Hey there Goldilocks,
What do you do?

I can't answer now,
I've got a big flu.

Bradley Sewell (9)
St Lawrence's RC Primary School, Feltham

Poems

P oems are sweet
O r they're very neat
E very one of them rhymes
M ost of them, at least
S ometimes they're silly and sometimes they're sad.

Matthew Mealand (10)
St Lawrence's RC Primary School, Feltham

Football Crazy

When I was little,
Just after I started to talk,
I knew that one day,
I would kick a ball when I could walk.

When for Christmas, I got a ball,
I couldn't wait to kick it,
Or head it when I got tall,
Which would also keep me fit.

Now I am eleven and very fast,
I still love playing and having fun,
I know my love will always last,
For football and I will run and run.

In about ten years from now,
I hope to score a lot,
Playing on a big pitch, I'd go *wow*
And hope it would also be nice and hot.

Daniel Constable (11)
St Lawrence's RC Primary School, Feltham

Rainbow

Rainbows consist of red, rainbows consist of blue
I love rainbows and I guess you do too

Rainbows are fun, rainbows are bright
They bring us joy and colourful light

Rainbows come when there's sun and rain
But rainbows bring happiness and take away pain.

Rainbows bring a smile to my face
And everyone in the human race

Rainbows consist of red, rainbows consist of blue
I love rainbows and so do you!

Afia Adjapong (11)
St Lawrence's RC Primary School, Feltham

Anger

The colour is red
It feels like a big ball of fire
It reminds you of bad times
It smells like fire going up your nose
It looks like a house on fire
It sounds like thunder
It tastes like you're eating red-hot chillies.

Luke Shokar (8)
St Lawrence's RC Primary School, Feltham

Football

I love kicking the ball
Against my garden wall
Now I realise
The most important thing in my life
Football
Whether it's placing the perfect volley
Or hitting the immaculate strike
And don't tell me you've never dreamed
Of nut-megging Ronaldiniho
You are Ronaldiniho
You are Wayne Rooney
You just need to believe!

Sean Stacey (11)
St Lawrence's RC Primary School, Feltham

Laughter

Laughter is red like a clown's red nose
It sounds like a singing rose
It tastes like Sloppy Joe's
It smells like the salty sea
It looks like an angry bee
It feels like a night on the sea
It reminds me of the magic key.

James Parkhouse (8)
St Lawrence's RC Primary School, Feltham

Fun

Fun is yellow like the sun
It smells like pizza
It looks like people playing
It sounds like a bird singing
It tastes like fresh air
It feels like heat
It reminds me of love.

Olaf Blazewicz (8)
St Lawrence's RC Primary School, Feltham

Laughter

Laughter is the colour of green grass on a summer's day
It smells like a day on the sandy beach
It feels like a hot summer's day
It reminds me of the blue sea
Laughter sounds like children giggling
It looks like people telling jokes.

Elisabeth Martin (8)
St Lawrence's RC Primary School, Feltham

The Night Horse

It waits in darkness
A palomino shade
Galloping and trotting through the forest
An ariegeois breed
Galloping over golden leaves
Jumping over bushes
And cantering through shallow lakes
Never making a sound
And never prey to a wild animal.

Hope-Frances Ritchie (11)
St Lawrence's RC Primary School, Feltham

Five, Four, Three, Two, One . . . Rhyme

Five, four, three, two, one . . . rhyme
Rhyme to the rhythm,
Rhyme to the beat,
Clap your hands and stamp your feet.

If you want to rhyme then save your time
And grab a pen and paper.

Five, four, three, two, one . . . rhyme
Rhyme to the rhythm,
Rhyme to the beat,
Clap your hands and stamp your feet.

Tongue twisters,
Long twisters
And rhyming twisters too
There's one thing in common . . .

Five, four, three, two, one . . . rhyme
Rhyme to the rhythm,
Rhyme to the beat,
Clap your hands and stamp your feet!

Robyn Long (11)
St Lawrence's RC Primary School, Feltham

Watch Out For The Witches

Watch out for the witches,
Hairy, fat or small,
Watch out for the witches,
Watch out for them all.

They're flying on their broomsticks,
With their small black cats,
Some have warts on their noses
And they all wear pointy hats.

Some of them have scruffy hair
And some of them smell,
I won't ever try to annoy them,
Because some of them are from Hell.

And I think all that would give you a fright
But it's even worse if you see one late at night.

Mollie Lang (11)
St Lawrence's RC Primary School, Feltham

My Baby Brother

Sometimes he screams,
Sometimes he dreams,
Sometimes he plays,
Sometimes he'll gaze,
Sometimes he talks,
Sometimes he walks.

Sometimes he sits, sometimes he stands,
Sometimes he crawls on his knees and hands,
Sometimes he snuggles up with his teddy,
Sometimes he looks next door at Freddie,
Sometimes he seems very happy,
Sometimes he just needs a new nappy.

Sometimes he likes a ride on my back,
He's my baby brother and his name's Jack,
In his highchair he noisily eats,
In his cot he dribbles on the sheets,
Sometimes he looks ready to pounce,
But he's one of my brothers, that's what counts!

John Durrans (11)
St Lawrence's RC Primary School, Feltham

Space

Space is a wonderful thing,
So exciting and fun,
All those planets, all them stars,
Do aliens really live on Mars?
Do they think? Do they breathe?
Do they have hands? Do they have feet?
Nobody knows,
What do you think?

Danika Bacon (11)
St Lawrence's RC Primary School, Feltham

Chelsea

Chelsea are the best
Chelsea are the best
They wear a lion badge on their vest
If you come and see
You will agree
That Chelsea are the best
And they aren't the worst
Because we're first!

Matthew Stansby (11)
St Lawrence's RC Primary School, Feltham

Mum And Me

We went for a paddle along the edge of the sea
And Mum stooped down and picked up some shells for me,
Some were bumpy and some were smooth,
I found it really hard to choose,
We bought the newspaper and sweets from the shop
And decided to settle on the hilltop,
We had lunch at the restaurant around midday,
Then Mum asked for the bill to pay,
In the middle of the afternoon,
We went to the park,
Then we made our way home before it got dark,
I tried to fall asleep with all my might
Well, after all, it was nearly midnight!

Georgina Johnson (10)
St Lawrence's RC Primary School, Feltham

My Poem About . . .

S unday is my day, whether rain or shine
P laying football is the game where I spend my time
O n the pitch scoring goals in the mud
R eturning home, my front door, I do thud,
'T ake off them clothes and clean the floor,' says my mum
from behind the door
S hower time is then soon to be, then maybe, just maybe, some TV.

Ashley Morton (11)
St Lawrence's RC Primary School, Feltham

The Bad Story

The poem I tell you has a story
Though it has a bit of glory
Lots of people have a dream
But it turns to a lot of steam
The water they drink at the fountain
They have to climb to the top of the mountain.

Alexander Larson (11)
St Lawrence's RC Primary School, Feltham

Little Red Riding Hood

Just as Mr Wolf was about to leave
Of course, he had another trick up his sleeve,
He quickly put on Little Red Riding Hood's cloak
And ran swiftly through the deep, dark wood,
Arriving at Gran's bungalow . . .
He shouted, 'Hello! Hello!'
Out came Little Red Riding Hood's mum
And quickly disappeared into his tum.

Sabina Fashoda (9)
St Lawrence's RC Primary School, Feltham

Chocolate, Chocolate, Chocolate

Chocolate is yummy
It fills my big tummy,
If chocolate ran away
I would search all day,
So I'm going to tell you that chocolate tastes good
So give it a try,
Before I cry.

Put chocolate out of its misery
It tastes nice and fizzy
And one more thing to say
Before I run away,
Chocolate is yummy
And fills *my* big tummy!

Kelsey Watterson (10)
St Lawrence's RC Primary School, Feltham

Football

Football is fun
Football is fun
Football is fun for everyone
It's not fun if you get booked or sent off
In Rio the best footballer in the world was born
His name is *Ronaldinho!*
He is my favourite footballer!

Patrick O'Reilly (11)
St Lawrence's RC Primary School, Feltham

Which Witch Is Which?

Which witch is which?
Which witch is where?
Which witch has legs which are covered in hair?

Which witch is here?
Which witch has just been to visit the mayor?

The witches are making a potion
Say which witch will stir in the frogs' legs today?

Hullabaloo, hullabaloo,
Hickle-di-pickle-di
Come out now!
Poof!

Sarah Chichlowska (10)
St Lawrence's RC Primary School, Feltham

Sweets

Sweets are great
Sweets taste good
I love them
And I think you should
All different colours and sizes
Some are yummy
And some are chewy
All types for everybody
Hard ones and minty ones
Humbugs, I like those
Whatever the style, sweets are fine.

Joe Carter (10)
St Lawrence's RC Primary School, Feltham

Ode To A Shred Of Paper

Oh, hail the wondrous shred of paper!
I adore your exquisite structure!
You are my life!
My reigning monarch of utmost power!
How I tremble in your presence,
How I quake when you lay in my hand.

Oh, shred of paper!
How I can fold you endlessly!
How I can work masterpieces on you!
How I can rip you so neatly!
I envy your robin egg-white colour.

Oh, shred of paper!
How I can chuck you at my sister!

How I hail you!
Oh, shred of paper!

Sarah Arifi (10)
The Lady Eleanor Holles Junior School

Teddy

Roses are red
Violets are blue
I love you
And I think you love me too

Every time you come home
You collect me from my shelf
We act like little rascals
Me and you, we act like elves

Then one day the door opens wide
You've finally come home
But you don't come and collect me
I suddenly feel so alone

I'm dumped in a big black bag
Into empty blackness I stare
You used to loved me, oh so much
But now no one seems to care

Now I hate big bags
And I hate the colour black
I still love you a lot
But I don't think you love me back.

Lisa Asher (10)
The Lady Eleanor Holles Junior School

Some Don't

I have a house, some don't
I have a dinner each night, some don't
I have new clothes, some don't
I have a bed, some don't
I have parents, some don't

I have justice, some don't
I have free speech, some don't
I have good health, some don't
I have love, some don't
I have a chance, some don't

Why?

Katie Hearsum (11)
The Lady Eleanor Holles Junior School

The Constrictor

The boa constrictor,
Is a lovely pet.
It coils up when it sleeps,
Like a big thick rope.
Its scales feel
As smooth as silk,
Just watch out -
Don't stroke it near the head!
It can be as dangerous
As a lioness guarding her cubs,
But my one is friendly
He never would . . .
Aaarrrrrggggghhhh!

Magenta Merrony (10)
The Lady Eleanor Holles Junior School

An Ode To A Salt And Vinegar Crisp

Oh, wonderful crisp
My tastebuds salute you
Your crunchy skin has a lush texture
The vinegary taste, it slips down my throat
A flush of excitement and joy runs down me
When I crunch you!

Oh, magnificent crisp
You have a place in my heart
My body craves for your additives
I can honestly say I will never eat
Any other crisps, chocolate or sweets again
I will only ever eat you!

Oh, tasty crisp
I will never leave a crumb of you behind
All of your brilliant flavour will drop into my mouth
You are my true destiny!

Emma Ward (10)
The Lady Eleanor Holles Junior School

Blackbird

The playground's bare,
As bare as can be,
It's far too big for little old me,
Climbing on the climbing frame,
The monkey bars,
It's all the same,
Except for one thing -
There's no one.
No one on the swing,
No one on the slide,
No one on the roundabout,
Taking a dizzy ride.
I miss the jokes, the laughs, the fun,
I just want to play with someone.
Eventually the ghost bell rings,
Then suddenly a blackbird sings,
I wish I were a blackbird,
Flying high in the sky,
I wish I were a blackbird,
Flying high,
High,
High.

Georgia Galton-Ayling (10)
The Lady Eleanor Holles Junior School

Potatoes!

There was a young lady from Lille
Who had a pile of potatoes to peel
She fell off her stool
And felt such a fool
So she ordered a takeway meal.

Carys Batcup (11)
The Lady Eleanor Holles Junior School

Winter

W ild winds, coldly blow
I nside houses, fires glow
N ew winter coat, new winter hat
T wo muddy boots upon the mat
E very bird safe in its nest
R oaring fires - home to rest!

Emilie Sims (11)
The Lady Eleanor Holles Junior School

Exam Nerves

My palms they are a-sweating
My heart is beating fast
I have three hours ahead of me
How am I going to last?

I should now be an expert
I should know what to do
I should have learnt my lessons
And worked a bit harder too!

I know that I can do this
I tell myself each day
But it doesn't get any easier
No matter what they say!

How many have I done now?
It must be three or four
And don't even ask me
If I'd like to do two more!

I'm so close to the end now
Only one more page to go
And then I can get out of here
Do some chilling, don't you know!

That's it, the final whistle
That's it, the final blow
That's it, I'm done and finished
That's it, it's time to go!

Hayley Miller (10)
The Lady Eleanor Holles Junior School

Tropical Island

In my summer holiday I went to see
My great, great uncle, his name is Jimmy.
This Uncle Jimmy lives so far, far away,
On his tropical island, I went to stay.
This tropical island has everything you need,
That's a fact, whatever colour or creed.
It's got palm trees swaying in the breeze,
It's got coconuts hanging from the trees.
It's got gentle waters lapping against the sand,
Plus, he owns the whole land.
Yes, this tropical island is a brilliant creation,
The only problem is, it's all in my imagination!

Bethan George (10)
The Lady Eleanor Holles Junior School

Dreaming Through A Window

There was once a very special, magical window
Hidden away in the corner of an enchanted room.

A poor, hungry beggar stared through the window
And gazed in at an enormous feast, his mouth watered.

A little girl glimpsed through the window
And saw gorgeous China dolls dressed in fabulous outfits,
her eyes lit up.

A farmer glanced through the window
And surveyed his fields of golden corn, rippling in the breeze,
he smiled.

A dog bounded up to the window
And pressed his wet, pink nose up against the glass
He noticed a string of juicy sausages, the dog howled
and wagged his tail.

I wiped the window and all I could see
Was a smiling reflection of me.

Pippa Bale (11)
The Lady Eleanor Holles Junior School

The Death Of War

I wish when my children are born, they look up the meaning of war.
I wish not to hear a gunshot firing in the air and from my window
see a field of blood.
I wish to switch on the television and not see people dying
and injured in rebellion.
I wish not to see army ships flying through the black air
and down below people falling.
I wish not to enter an army training centre and be told my son
has gone to fight.
I wish not to see my children come home from school early
and run into a shelter.
I wish about all things to do with peace and I wish peace
would be restored.
I wish all stories and poems are about happiness and the word war
is not mentioned.
I wish not to see men walking in the street dressed in green
and carrying weapons.
I wish war will never be a thing we train for again.

Simerhan Hunjunt (10)
The Lady Eleanor Holles Junior School

I Like Going To The Zoo

I like going to the zoo,
There's so much to see and do,
Let's look at the animals (let's hope they aren't asleep)
Peer through the bars of their cages, have a little peep.

I like the cheeky chimps
And penguins eating shrimps,
I like the beautiful tigers, majestic and proud,
Animals watch from their cages, they're watching the crowd.

Swinging gibbons - a wonderful sight!
Could that be a baby? It just might!
The baby animals are just *so cute!*
Some animals are so amazing, they leave you mute.

The lemurs are screeching, it hurts my ears,
Let's go to the shop and buy souvenirs,
Suddenly, it's time to go,
That's not fair! I'm filled with woe.

But is the zoo really such a wonderful place?
How would *you* like to be stuck in an enclosed space?
Shouldn't animals be free to roam,
In the jungle, the mountains, their own home?

Sarah Metcalf (11)
Twickenham Preparatory School